PHILIPPIANS

Brief Thoughts for Busy People

LISA MCHEARD

First Printing: 2020

lisamcheard@gmail.com

To the Great Cloud of Witnesses reflected in every word of this book. Thank you for sharing your love of God's Word with me. (Hebrews 12:1)

PHILIPPIANS 1:1

Paul and Timothy, servants of Christ Jesus, To all God's holy people in Christ Jesus at Philippi, together with the overseers and deacons

---

Assimilation is convenient, but it is disgraceful from a Gospel standpoint. Camouflage the Spirit of Christ in us, and the likelihood of engaging in conversations about our faith evaporates, and our witness wanes (Matthew 5:16). This approach protects us from uncomfortable questions and helps us fly under the radar. But it does nothing to challenge inaccurate ideas about God or display the image of Christ in us.

The book of Philippians addresses braver folks, holy people whose conversations and choices set them apart (Philippians 2:12-13). They gave sacrificially to support Paul's work with other churches (Philippians 4:15), loved one another, and looked for ways to support the downtrodden and downcast among them. The Philippian believers stood out because they were less like those who lived around them and more like Jesus (Philippians 2:14-16).

We, like the Philippians, are called to be brave and holy in a world whose default response is the rejection of unusual ideas. Our approach to life should stand out from the ordinary (1 Peter 2:9). Instead of hiding the hope within us, God expects us to display it boldly. Committed to the propagation of the Gospel, we are meant to live distinctive lives and share extraordinary Truth for God's glory and not our own (1 Peter 2:12).

PHILIPPIANS 1:2

*Grace and peace to you from God our Father
and the Lord Jesus Christ.*

God graciously leans toward us to bestow all the benefits of Christ on us. (Ephesians 3:6) He pours spiritual blessings on us with the willing, generous attention of a loving father toward his children. His attentiveness is a benevolence we depend on and a benefit without which we cannot survive. The truth that God is leaning toward us and not away is a game-changer. We no longer need to fear his retribution for our sins. He lavishes grace upon us through Christ, who offered himself as a substitutionary sacrifice to earn God's favor for us (Isaiah 53:6).

God commits to our wholeness. He does not promise a complete absence from troubles, but His peace and steadiness amid them. In the brokenness of a fallen world, we are unbroken because God broke Jesus for us. In the throes of conflict, we are confident because he has already overcome them. (John 16:33)

God fills us to overflowing with grace and peace and urges us to spill grace and peace as generously on those around us. We aren't sponges meant to sop it up until someone squeezes us. We are pitchers meant to constantly decant God's blessings to others, in acknowledgment of his generous provision in our lives. (2 Peter 1:3-8)

PHILIPPIANS 1:3-5

I thank my God every time I remember you. In all my prayers for all of you, I always pray with joy because of your partnership in the gospel from the first day until now

The world urges us to live autonomous lives expending our energies in competition for recognition and reward. But God calls us to unite as an interdependent, active whole (John 17:22-23), combining our resources and fully supporting one another as we work toward God's goals and not selfish ones. The unified generosity of the Philippians inspired thankfulness and joy in Paul. Even at a distance, they connected with him and supplied his daily needs so he could work to advance the Gospel without distraction.

Our abundant blessings are not earned but bestowed by the lavish grace of God and are not for our benefit alone, no matter what we hear every day. Society encourages us to hold our blessings selfishly, with a "me first, then you" attitude. But God's grace floods our lives so it can spill over into the lives of those around us. God pours out heavenly blessings for us to invest in ways that produce eternal gain and inspire thankfulness and joy in others (Matthew 25:14-30). The combination of our resources facilitates extraordinary generosity and strengthens Gospel activity in our families, neighborhoods, cities, and around the world.

PHILIPPIANS 1:6

Being confident of this, that he who began a good work in you will carry it on to completion until the day of Christ Jesus.

Some people believe that God set the world in motion, then walked away. They assume that unconcerned with the details of daily life; he leaves us to our own devices. How ridiculous!

The Bible puts that false conclusion to rest. God knows us before we are born. (Psalm 139:16) He fashions us to fulfill a specific purpose. (Ephesians 2:10) He begins a good work in us before we can recognize his hand of influence in our lives

It is not our strength or smarts that keep us on the straight and narrow. It is God's steadfast faithfulness. We have a capricious commitment, inconsistent actions, and unreliable emotions. But God is never fickle. He is never erratic or unstable. He is never distracted by circumstances but is attentive, constant, persistent, and steady. Thomas Watson put it beautifully: "If once God's electing love rises upon the soul, it never sets."

What comfort when we grow tired and fed up with the struggle against sin. We may falter, but God stays the course (2 Timothy 2:13).

PHILIPPIANS 1:7

It is right for me to feel this way about all of you, since I have you in my heart and, whether I am in chains or defending and confirming the gospel, all of you share in God's grace with me.

The word for "defending" in this verse is apologia. It doesn't mean arguing a person into belief but presenting a well-reasoned case that attracts them to the truth. We can't accomplish that if we don't do our research. Defending the Gospel requires a foundation of Scriptural understanding (2 Timothy 3:16-17) obtained through diligent effort (2 Timothy 2:15).

The word for "confirming" means walking on solid ground. It reminds us that the way we live out the truth of the Gospel in everyday life matters as much as what we say about it. (Ephesians 2:10) Our witness for Christ is most effective when we operate as if we believe what we say about him. (Ephesians 4:22-24)

As we speak and live God's Truth, the demonstration of his grace through us attracts others. But there's a flip side to that coin. If our speech and actions are worldly, then we steal grace from those around us (Matthew 5:13). We are conduits of God's favor in the world.

PHILIPPIANS 1:8

God can testify how I long for all of you with
the affection of Christ Jesus.

Christ-like affection is instinctual compassion that flows from the depths of Gospel love and moves us to act thoughtfully toward others. It is the outplay of the selflessness Christ modeled for us when he walked the earth and a reflection of the kindness he showed.

Christ-like affection sees the best in someone and not the worst. (Luke 7:44-47) It chooses forgiveness for the sake of the Gospel and doesn't keep a tally sheet of relational debits and credits (1 Corinthians 13:5). It shows compassion to unlovable people because Christ showed compassion to unlovable us. (John 13:34)

Affection like this reaches deep to find the strength to remain faithful during difficult relational trials and trusts God's promise to reward those who persevere in difficult circumstances. (Hebrews 6:10)

PHILIPPIANS 1:9-10

And this is my prayer: that your love may abound more and more in knowledge and depth of insight, so that you may be able to discern what is best and may be pure and blameless for the day of Christ

---

God requires our love for one another to exceed ordinary love. If ordinary love is patient, then our love perseveres through even the most trying of circumstances. If it is kind, then our love goes above and beyond kindness to sacrifice personal comfort for the good of someone else. Gospel love gushes. It does not trickle.

The only way we can sustain that kind of personal expenditure is by immersing ourselves in the perfect, indefatigable love of God. He pours in, so we don't dry up. (Romans 5:5) He generously supplies what we need so that we can generously attend to the needs of others. (2 Corinthians 9:10) He gives more grace so that we can always be gracious. (2 Peter 1:2)

The degree to which we grasp God's love for us is the degree to which we can love those He places in our path each day. The current of our love increases, the more our knowledge of God does. It is strongest when we take the time to study his Word and meet with him in prayer – plunging ourselves into the wellspring of God's rich character before we try to reach the world. (2 Peter 1:3)

PHILIPPIANS 1:11

Filled with the fruit of righteousness that comes through Jesus Christ—to the glory and praise of God.

Discouragement is one of Satan's most effective weapons against us. He wants us to feel empty. He schemes to keep us focused on perceived holes in our Christian walk and sparks shame in us because of them. He pokes and prods at our Gospel commitment until we collapse thirsty and dry (1 Peter 5:8).

Thankfully, God doesn't sprinkle when he attends to our spiritual thirst; he pours (John 4:10-14). As members of his heavenly household, we are drenched in benefits (Psalm 103:2-5). Paul understood this, and his prayer was that the Philippians would grow to understand it too.

God doesn't deal in emptiness or shame. Jesus took care of all that on the Cross. God lavishes grace upon us because he has fully forgiven us through his Son (1 Peter 2:24). There's no residual anger on his part. He looks at us and sees Jesus. The same love God has for him stuffs our empty spots until there is no room for humiliation or disgrace, only joy, peace, and abundant hope (Romans 15:13).

PHILIPPIANS 1:12-13

Now I want you to know, brothers and sisters, that what has happened to me has actually served to advance the gospel. As a result, it has become clear throughout the whole palace guard and to everyone else that I am in chains for Christ.

If we are not careful, we operate under the worldly idea that our good works protect us from the hard things in life. We spend our time trying to keep the scales of justice balanced in our favor and see hard situations as punishment for our failure to live up to God's perfect standards. The idea that God weighs our good and bad before he blesses us is unhealthy and untrue. (Ephesians 2:8)

God's grace has nothing to do with our behavior and everything to do with Christ's. Jesus paid every bit of the sin debt we owed God by dying on the Cross. We are beneficiaries of his perfect righteousness. God's favor does not depend on our thoughts, words, or actions, but the perfect obedience of Jesus. (Romans 5:1-2)

Such truth transforms us from fear-based performers to authentic followers, gratefully displaying our devotion to him (Titus 3:3-8). Our most difficult moments become opportunities to advance the Gospel instead of retribution for imperfect behavior. Christ's sacrifice frees us to communicate the rich glory of living every moment, good or bad, as beneficiaries of God's overwhelming grace.

PHILIPPIANS 1:14

And because of my chains, most of the brothers and sisters have become confident in the Lord and dare all the more to proclaim the gospel without fear.

The people around us are searching for safety as the world around them shifts and shakes. They long for a moment of peace, the deep, restorative breath of being able to count on something for the long haul. Overwhelmed by uncertainty and disappointed by lies, they ache to stand on solid ground.

The witness of just one Christian, standing confidently on the sure foundation of God's promises, is difficult to ignore. (2 Timothy 2:19) Steadfast trust and the strength of the Spirit are a powerful combination! Such courage doesn't guarantee a comfortable life. Paul experienced beating, stoning, and imprisonment because of his devotion to the Gospel (2 Timothy 3:10-11). But his example inspired bravery and commitment in others.

Just one of us resolved to lead, willing to share, bold enough to ford the groundswells of uncertainty - one reliable person - dug in, immovable, and holding tightly to the promise of eternal life (1 Timothy 6:12) is what it takes to lead our struggling neighbors to the safe and stable ground beneath the Cross. (1 Corinthians 15:58

PHILIPPIANS 1:15-17

It is true that some preach Christ out of envy and rivalry, but others out of goodwill. The latter do so out of love, knowing that I am put here for the defense of the gospel. The former preach Christ out of selfish ambition, not sincerely, supposing that they can stir up trouble for me while I am in chains.

Be wary of speakers who add to the simple proclamation of God's Word to benefit themselves. Stay away from churches that toe the "party line" to the point that they deride others who are preaching faithfully but aren't part of the same denomination. If a speaker spends even a moment glorifying his part of God's Kingdom at the expense of another, then he is sinning. (Titus 3:9-11)

Preaching is not a means of proving one man's grasp of God's Word over another's. Nor is it an opportunity for the amplification of any personal point of view. None of us has a perfect one of those. We all have sinned and fall short of God's glory. (Romans 3:23)

The unity of the Church is a primary focus of Christ's message. (John 17:22-23) God expects us to work together as a cohesive body of believers because we walk in the world on his behalf.

PHILIPPIANS 1:18A

But what does it matter? The important thing is that in every way,
whether from false motives or true, Christ is preached.
And because of this I rejoice.

Have you ever been afraid to tell someone about Jesus because you might get it wrong? Take encouragement from this verse. Paul reminds us that the important thing is that Christ is preached, not perfection in how we do it.

Paul believed in the power of the essential message of the Gospel: that Christ died for our sins, was buried, and then was raised from the dead (1 Corinthians 15:3-4). He understood that the effectiveness of our witness rests in the power of God's message and not how we proclaim it (1 Corinthians 3:7). The potential for Gospel transformation is released any time anyone proclaims Gospel Truth.

We forget that. We fasten on our bells and whistles. We add our fluff and show, intending to entice others by our delivery. But it is God's promise of salvation that has the power to save and not our ways and means (1 Peter 3:15).

PHILIPPIANS 1:18B-19

Yes, and I will continue to rejoice, for I know that through your prayers and God's provision of the Spirit of Jesus Christ what has happened to me will turn out for my deliverance.

Distress is a part of this imperfect life. We can't get away from it. When man rebelled against God, the consequences of his choice became our constant companions (Romans 5:12). Things like sickness, death, hatred, and competition started in the Garden and continue because of our disobedience and rebellion. They are the brutal result of sin (Ephesians 2:1-3).

But God didn't leave us to face sin's hardship alone. He sent his Son, who conquered sin and death. Because of Jesus Christ, the consequences of sin don't have the same relentless power to discourage and dismay (Ephesians 2:4-5). We have a sinless eternity ahead of us, and a steadfast companion while we live out our earthly days. Jesus left the Holy Spirit to strengthen and encourage us in our distress (John 14:16-17).

We also have the company of other Christians, who like us, are traveling toward Heaven. As we set aside our sinful habits toward one another for godly ones, sin's consequences lose their power to dismay. When love, support, humility, and prayer become our default, we all become a little stronger and more joyful in the struggle (Colossians 3:12-16).

PHILIPPIANS 1:20

I eagerly expect and hope that I will in no way be ashamed but will have sufficient courage so that now as always Christ will be exalted in my body, whether by life or by death.

God's unshakeable promises are our earnest expectation and confidence. We can trust his character no matter what trials we endure (Lamentations 3:22). Our courage flows from Christ's example of faithfulness and not any inner strength or mettle of our own (Hebrews 12:2-3), and we accomplish God's Will by the power of the Holy Spirit (Romans 8:11). We are not in this alone!

Fear overwhelms when we allow ourselves to glance past the strong back of the Savior, who fords a path through every trial, to the challenges we see ahead (Deuteronomy 31:8). We get lost in the weeds of "what-if," while he calls us to follow in his sure and steady footprints. It's through faithful obedience that God is exalted and not showy bravado (Zechariah 4:6).

Courage to face any trial, even death, with confidence grows as we begin to understand this truth. Hard things are bearable in the company of the Savior, who is not surprised, alarmed, or overwhelmed by anything.

PHILIPPIANS 1:21

For to me, to live is Christ and to die is gain.

Conventional wisdom tells us to live for ourselves. The media bombards us with schemes to fulfill our deepest desires and fondest dreams. The idea of expending precious energy on something other than personal happiness is bizarre in the eyes of the world. But God offers so much more to followers of Christ.

He offers unrestrained faith and the echo of Christ in every moment and experience. He sets down deliberate steps for the sake of the Gospel and saturates our hearts with the desire to know Christ and to help others know Christ too. (2 Corinthians 2:14)

Death is gain for the Christian. The promise of spending eternity with God sets fire to our ministry. God's promises are certain, and we can set our hope upon them (2 Corinthians 1:20). There is no need to fear death because death means uniting with our Savior forever (1 Corinthians 15:57).

PHILIPPIANS 1:22

If I am to go on living in the body, this will mean fruitful labor for me. Yet what shall I choose? I do not know!

For as long as we breathe, our goal as Christians is fruitful labor for the glory of God. We are the branches of the Vine sent out into the world by God to bear much fruit (John 15:5). Everything else we do is secondary to the cultivation of the Gospel in the lives of those around us (Colossians 1:10).

We don't need to search for opportunities to share Gospel Truth. God prepared good works in advance for us (Ephesians 2:10). We need to be ready and willing to reach where he points and do what He commands us to do (1 Peter 3:15).

So, we send out wispy shoots of kindness, encouragement, and hope as we interact with others, trusting that they will furrow deep into hurting, searching, discouraged hearts. We do it faithfully until the shoots take root. Then we share the reason we are growing at all – the living giving, heart-healing gift of Gospel Grace (Colossians 4:5-6).

PHILIPPIANS 1:23-24

---

*I am torn between the two: I desire to depart and be with Christ,
which is better by far; but it is more necessary for you
that I remain in the body.*

There is a natural longing in the children of God to be home with him (2 Corinthians 5:6-8). We grow weary of struggling with the consequences of sin and eager for rest from worldly striving. If we are not careful, that longing can lead to discouragement as we see evil growing in influence (1 Peter 5:8).

God intended the world he created to be a permanent home for humans. But humans rejected his plan and opened the garden gate to sin (Romans 5:12). We will struggle with the consequences of that invitation for as long as we dwell on this earth (John 16:33).

But God rescues us from this hopeless situation. He provides an eternal escape from sin in the life, death, and resurrection of Jesus Christ (Romans 5:15), then assigns the task of sharing that Good News while we remain here. Then, when we have completed the assignment, he ushers us into His glorious presence, and we experience the fulfillment of all he ever promised (Psalm 145:13)

Come quickly, Lord Jesus!

PHILIPPIANS 1:25-26

Convinced of this, I know that I will remain, and I will continue with all of you for your progress and joy in the faith. So that through my being with you again your boasting in Christ Jesus will abound on account of me.

Every effort one of us makes to share the Gospel joins us to the efforts of our brothers and sisters in Christ (1 Thessalonians 4:9-10). There are no lone wolves or solitary soldiers. We are all in this together. Unity is key to the advancement of God's Kingdom, and unselfish collaboration inspires cooperative joy in the faith (Ephesians 4:1-5).

We falter when we focus too narrowly on our priorities and accomplishments at the expense of the work and reputation of others. We are not in competition against one another, but on a Spirit-directed journey toward the same goal (1 Corinthians 12:4-6).

Just as the Philippians had a reason for proud confidence because of Paul's faithfulness to the Gospel, we should express proud confidence in Christ's work of faithfulness through one another. Our love and unity are what distinguishes us from the world (John 13:35).

PHILIPPIANS 1:27

Whatever happens, conduct yourselves in a manner worthy of the gospel of Christ. Then, whether I come and see you or only hear about you in my absence, I will know that you stand firm in the one Spirit, striving together as one for the faith of the gospel

The most effective church is a body of believers so committed to one another in conversation and conduct that it seems as if they breathe in unison. (Acts 4:32-33) They think the same thoughts about sharing the Gospel and work shoulder to shoulder to accomplish it. There are no factions, no backroom complaining, no pushiness, or manipulation. (Ephesians 4:29-32) They show forth God's glory in a manner worthy of the truth they proclaim, as a habit, not a coincidence, and are too busy working for God to work against each other. (2 Peter 1:3)

The most effective church recognizes that words and actions are heavenly currency. They do not squander their capital by operating in a way that discredits their witness. They grow the treasure of their heavenly holdings by investing every conversation and activity in ways that point others to the Savior. Their example authenticates their message. (Ephesians 5:1-2)

PHILIPPIANS 1:28

Without being frightened in any way by those who oppose you.
This is a sign to them that they will be destroyed, but that you will
be saved—and that by God.

Fear paralyzes. It robs us of initiative and isolates us from others. Gospel hope enlivens (1 Peter 1:3-5.) It draws us together by the power of the Holy Spirit in us, the same spirit who raised Jesus from the dead (Romans 8:11). The strength of the opposition may overwhelm us at times, but it can never overcome us because we are united in Christ (Ephesians 1:3-10).

Unity equals strength – strength of message, strength of purpose, and strength of resolve. Brothers and sisters in Christ standing shoulder to shoulder for the Gospel is a formidable sight. Such harmony is hard to ignore. It makes the opposition take notice, shakes their doggedness and causes the undecided to wonder if they missed something (John 4:39-42)

PHILIPPIANS 1:29-30

For it has been granted to you on behalf of Christ not only to believe in him, but also to suffer for him, since you are going through the same struggle you saw I had, and now hear that I still have.

So much of what we consider suffering for Christ is just experiencing the consequences of living in a fallen world or enduring the fallout for our brash and arrogant behavior in the public arena. We point fingers and judge others loudly then are surprised when they push back.

Real suffering for Christ is more than having a heated discussion with the opposition or reading rude replies to our social media posts. Real suffering for Christ means experiencing the loss of our livelihood, our freedom to speak, or even our lives for the sake of the Gospel (John 15:19). Paul understood the cost of proclaiming the Gospel in a hostile environment, and he considered it a privilege to suffer the consequences.

Today there are Christians in other parts of the world who experience real suffering for their Christian witness. Churches burn. Pastors sit in prison. People die because they boldly live out their faith. That is real suffering on behalf of Christ, and they need our prayers for peace, protection, and the freedom to worship without fear (John 16:33).

PHILIPPIANS 2:1-2

Therefore if you have any encouragement from being united with Christ, if any comfort from his love, if any common sharing in the Spirit, if any tenderness and compassion, then make my joy complete by being like-minded, having the same love, being one in spirit and of one mind.

Christ joins us to himself (Ephesians 2:13), and so we experience the comfort of his perfect love (1 John 4:18) and share in the power of the Holy Spirit (Ephesians 1:17-20). The effect of these generous benefits should be sacrificial love for others, unity of thought, and singleness of purpose.

Such a heavenly perspective of daily life is entirely opposed to the worldly view, which permeates our minds and tricks us into believing that individuality, competition, and power over others is our primary goal. (1 Corinthians 2:14)

But God expects Christians to think differently. The foundational commitment of Christian life is others-focused. It is one Christian at a time caring for one Christian at a time, so we meet every need and can all be about our Father's business without the distraction of worldly concerns. Look at the words Paul uses here: united, sharing, like-minded, one spirit, and mind. The goal of the Church is community, not individuality. (Acts 4:32)

PHILIPPIANS 2:3-4

Do nothing out of selfish ambition or vain conceit. Rather, in humility value others above yourselves, not looking to your own interests but each of you to the interests of the others.

Every small act of humility is a larger act of trust. When we let go of control, we exercise faith that God is at work in this world and other lives besides our own.

Jesus is the perfect example of this. He humbled himself because he trusted the Father completely. He held fast to the faith that everything God promised would come to fruition at the right time and sacrificed his desires for the redemption of others, even when those around him acted selfishly. (Hebrews 12:2)

When we set aside our comfort and desires for the good of someone else, we can be sure God notices (Hebrews 6:10). We don't need to worry that our efforts are lost or wonder if anyone sees our sacrifice. God does, and he never lets an act of compassion, grace, or self-sacrifice go unrewarded. (Proverbs 11:18)

PHILIPPIANS 2:5

*In your relationships with one another, have
the same mindset as Christ Jesus.*

Jesus had no pretense or insincerity. His inner life matched his
outward actions. He never put on airs or tried to be something he
was not. He set his mind on glorifying God. He filled his thought
life with God's Word until obedience was as natural as breathing.
That doesn't mean it was easy. But Jesus understood his outward
witness began in his heart and mind.

There is Scriptural evidence of this recorded in the account of
Christ's Temptation in Luke 4. God's Word was the armor that
guarded him against the lusts of the flesh (Luke 4:3-4). God's
Word shielded him from the lusts of the eye (Luke 4:5-8). God's
Word was the tether that kept him from falling into the pride of life
(Luke 4:9-12).

Jesus modeled the power of faithful study and application of God's
Word. His walk matched his talk, and that drew people to him.
Imagine the witness we could have in the world if we all did the
same. (Ephesians 5:1-2)

PHILIPPIANS 2:6-7

Who, being in very nature God, did not consider equality with God something to be used to his own advantage; rather, he made himself nothing by taking the very nature of a servant, being made in human likeness.

Jesus, being God, could have conquered sin and death by his infinite strength and authority. But what would that have taught us? Instead, he became one of us, submitting his rights as the second person of the Trinity for our sake. He, the radiance of God's glory and the exact representation of his being, who participated in the creation of the world (Hebrews 1:3), emptied himself to show us the Father.

That's a strange idea to people who spend most of their time trying to get ahead (1 Corinthians 1:18). We push against one another, fighting for position and belittling others to win our place. We live myopic lives, so engrossed with our spot on the canvas that we miss the broad sweeping brushstrokes of God's love and grace.

Jesus left eternity so we could experience eternal life (Galatians 4:4-5). He made himself nothing so we could gain everything (Matthew 20:28), sacrificing his life solely to save us (Romans 8:3-4). He set the only real example of Gospel living for us to emulate - emptying ourselves to serve others (1 Peter 4:10).

PHILIPPIANS 2:8

And being found in appearance as a man, he humbled himself by becoming obedient to death—even death on a cross!

A genuinely humble life is empty of self and full of God's grace. It overflows with the Fruit of the Spirit. (Galatians 5:22-23) Humility reflects God's love by preferring his will above its own. It rejoices in the richness of God's good grace. Humility displays wholeness in a world that urges us to break one another to pieces. It allows us to be
long-tempered toward others rather than flying off the handle (Ephesians 4:2) and fits us for God's Work. It instills inherent good nature in us that draws people to our message (Acts 2:46-47).

Humility grows our confidence in the promises of God and decreases our reliance on worldly commendation. It fills us with a quiet strength that radiates authority but does not announce it. Humility allows the Spirit to have mastery over our thoughts, desires, and attitudes (Romans 7:5-6).

The foundation of authentic humility is death – death to personal magnification, death to inter-personal competitiveness, death to selfishness. Humility is the primary evidence of the authenticity of our commitment to Christ (Romans 6:11).

PHILIPPIANS 2:9-11

*Therefore God exalted him to the highest place and gave him the
name that is above every name, that at the name of Jesus every
knee should bow, in heaven and on earth and under the earth,
and every tongue acknowledge that Jesus Christ is Lord,
to the glory of God the Father.*

We tend to shy away from the hard truths in Scripture. It's more comfortable to speak of God in general terms that focus on his goodness, kindness, and grace rather than teach the whole counsel of Scripture, which includes his holiness, right to rule, and judgment.

There will be a day when every knee shall bow at the name of Jesus, either in thankful celebration or in trembling disgrace. The Bible clearly states that those who acknowledge him as Savior and Lord will experience the overwhelming joy of God's Great Promise fulfilled (Matthew 16:26-27) and that those who rejected him will feel unequivocal shame as they recognize their stubborn ignorance. (2 Thessalonians 1:8-9)

Faith is not a game. God promises life to those who commit to obedience and death to those who don't. He lavishes incredible benefits on those who believe (Psalm 103:2-5). But he guarantees brokenness and eternal separation to those who do not (Isaiah 1:28). There are no two ways about it!

PHILIPPIANS 2:12

Therefore, my dear friends, as you have always obeyed—not only in my presence, but now much more in my absence—continue to work out your salvation with fear and trembling.

We cannot be who God wants us to be without his constant help. Sin tinges even our best intentions. We may look gracious and self-sacrificing, but more often than not, our thoughts and intentions are less than pure (Jeremiah 17:9). In the context of humility, a healthy dose of fear and trembling at our frequent failure to meet God's standard and our need for rescue from ourselves is a good thing (Psalm 32:5).

We cannot accomplish any good work without God's Good Grace. He plants the seed of desire to please him within us (Ephesians 2:10). The Holy Spirit nurtures and empowers us. Our only contribution to the whole thing is a willingness to obey - to rest in his knowledge of a given situation and move forward even when our hearts are resistant to the assignment, emulating Jesus as we go (Jude 1:24-25).

PHILIPPIANS 2:13

---

*For it is God who works in you to will and to act
in order to fulfill his good purpose.*

God instills the intention to act on behalf of His good pleasure, and then He energizes our efforts. He directs the current and not the other way around (Ephesians 2:10). When we get that backward, we grow weary and discouraged. A conduit without power flowing through it is just an empty pipe.

Any desire to love or serve is a direct result of godly inspiration. We can't depend on our natural selves. Left to our own devices, we are selfish, arrogant, and lazy (Romans 7:23). But God doesn't leave us to our own devices. He steadily removes any self-sufficient ideas we might have and nudges us toward acts that bring him glory.

The thought of someone that pops into our heads, that idea of how to minister grace, the impulse to do something that would put a smile on someone else's face are all invitations from God waiting for a response. Our days are filled with opportunities if we pay attention to God's prodding. (Hebrews 13:20-21)

PHILIPPIANS 2:14

Do everything without grumbling or arguing

What I say, whether under my breath or aloud, reveals the condition of my heart. My grumbling exposes anger, frustration, pride, and greed (Proverbs 13:10). I want what I don't have, and my dissatisfaction reveals itself in my muttering. Then muttering becomes a private pity party. I indulge in righteous indignation while assigning impure motives to others, where there are none (Matthew 7:1-2). My faulty reasoning betrays me. And most awful of all, I begin to reflect worldliness instead of godliness.

Since godliness with contentment is most Christ-like (1 Timothy 6:6), then my response to frustration and disappointment should be different. Compassion, kindness, humility, gentleness, and patience should be my heart language (Colossians 3:12). My contribution in any situation should reflect love, joy, and peace. (Galatians 5:22-23) Then my conversation will stand in stark contrast to the worldly norm and draw others to the Gospel (Colossians 4:5-6).

PHILIPPIANS 2:15–16A

So that you may become blameless and pure, "children of God
without fault in a warped and crooked generation.
Then you will shine among them like stars in the sky
as you hold firmly to the word of life.

There is a pall of warped and crooked ideology that hangs over our
world (2 Corinthians 4:4). It grows increasingly heavy as we stray
further and further away from God. Whenever man puts himself in
the center of things, death follows - the end of reason, real
purpose, and cooperation toward a worthy goal. We are in danger
of suffocating under the weight of self-centered sin. (1 John 1:5–6)

God's truth picks away at the heavy cloth of discouragement and
misdirection, making tiny holes for light to shine through. We are
the light (1 Thessalonians 5:5). We become navigation points for
the lost around us, as we hold firmly to the truth. And the more we
shine, the larger the holes grow until the pall begins to shred, and
lost people step blinking from the darkness of sin to the bright
hope of the Gospel. (Matthew 5:14–16)

PHILIPPIANS 2:16B

*And then I will be able to boast on the day of Christ
that I did not run or labor in vain.*

Gospel living is not just a distraction from worldly concerns, but our primary daily focus (1 Peter 2:9). It's not something we give attention to for a couple of hours each Sunday. It is the foundation of our behavior every day of the week (Titus 2:14). God's Word should permeate every conversation and action in which we engage. Holding forth the Word of Life is a serious, eternally important business! God's message, through us, allows sinners who are dead in sin to become alive in Christ (Ephesians 2:5-6).

If we profess faith in Jesus Christ, then we automatically accept God's call to proclaim hope to others, not as a leisure time activity, but as a vocation (Ephesians 5:8-10). Every bit of effort we expend, whether at our secular workplaces or sitting in the coffee shop down the street, is an investment in eternity. This heavenly perspective changes us and through us changes the world.

PHILIPPIANS 2:17–18

But even if I am being poured out like a drink offering on the sacrifice and service coming from your faith, I am glad and rejoice with all of you. So you too should be glad and rejoice with me.

Paul recognized that the essence of the Gospel is laying down one's life for others (John 15:13). He willingly sacrificed personal freedom and comfort so that as many people as possible could experience redemption through Jesus Christ. (2 Corinthians 6:3–10) He didn't waste time complaining about how difficult things were. He fixed his eyes on Jesus and seized every opportunity to proclaim Christ's saving power. (Hebrews 12:2)

Paul's goal was not financial security or social standing. Antagonism didn't threaten him. He trusted that God would meet his needs as he poured himself out for the Gospel (2 Corinthians 9:8). Trust like that goes against our modern sensibilities. Pragmatic as we are, we rationalize a hasty retreat the moment Gospel ministry requires too much sacrifice. But Gospel ministry is hardly ever logical. It often requires us to do things that don't make worldly sense (1 Corinthians 1:27). Paul's example reminds us that there is no such thing as giving too much when it comes to sharing Christ (Galatians 2:20).

PHILIPPIANS 2:19-20

I hope in the Lord Jesus to send Timothy to you soon, that I also may be cheered when I receive news about you. I have no one else like him, who will show genuine concern for your welfare.

This verse reminds us that there is no such thing as a solitary Christian. The Church is the Body of Christ and has many parts, each necessary for accomplishing God's Will (1 Corinthians 12:12-20). Independent thought and separation from fellowship weaken a person's Christian walk. We are all in this together! (Romans 12:4-5)

Attending worship connects us to Christ in a way that standing alone cannot. For a short time, we are together focusing on something other than our own ideas and importance. We stand shoulder to shoulder with brothers and sisters who have experienced the same great Gift we have and who share the same desire to know Christ and make him known.

Serving with other Christians expands our perspective and makes our efforts efficient. Our combined gifts bring God glory in a way that we can't individually. (Hebrews 10:24-25)

PHILIPPIANS 2:21

For everyone looks out for their own interests,
not those of Jesus Christ.

Our primary focus should be on the things that Christ deems significant and not our interests. But what are the essential things, according to Jesus? The Sermon on the Mount is an excellent place to start.

Jesus is concerned with character, the outward display of a heart committed to God (Matthew 5:3-12). He desires a recognizable witness in the world (Matthew 5:13-20). Christ wants forgiveness to be our habitual response to any offense (Matthew 5:21-26) and unshakeable commitment and respect for one another to be the hallmark of our witness. He requires truth and generosity in our dealings with one another (Matthew 5:33-42) and uncommon love toward everyone, especially those who are hardest to love (Matthew 5:43-48).

If our priorities line up with these, we bring glory and honor to God. But when individual tastes and interests eclipse Christ's concerns, we fail in our witness for him.

PHILIPPIANS 2:22-23

But you know that Timothy has proved himself, because as a son with his father he has served with me in the work of the gospel. Therefore I hope to send him immediately, as soon as I see how things go with me.

Ministry is a lonely row to hoe. People tend to make assumptions about how full-time servants of Christ spend their time and expect that others are taking care of their needs. So those who dedicate their lives entirely to the Gospel can feel isolated and overlooked (2 Timothy 1:15).

Timothy recognized Paul's need for consistent, dependable support. He served with Paul as he traveled and preached (1 Thessalonians 1:1), stood shoulder to shoulder with him during his most difficult trials, and was imprisoned with Paul (Hebrews 13:23). Paul trusted Timothy and sent him as a personal representative when he was unable to visit struggling churches (Acts 19:22). Timothy ministered to Paul and for him so that Paul could concentrate on the work God sent him to do. (2 Timothy 4:7)

PHILIPPIANS 2:24

And I am confident in the Lord that I myself will come soon.

Here, bookmarked between Timothy and Epaphroditus, Paul expresses his intent to visit the Philippians in person. He struggled with his distance from them and longed to spend more time sharing the Gospel and enjoying their company. Loneliness and separation affect strong, faithful men of God too!

But Paul wasn't paralyzed by his lonely state. He practiced content in all situations, even prison because he trusted God to do more than he could ever ask or imagine (Ephesians 3:20). Present challenges were no match for the good works God assigned (Ephesians 2:10), and physical limitations did not diminish Paul's hope.

There's a lesson there for us. The key to overcoming loneliness and limitations is focus. As we concentrate on Gospel priorities, we experience hope that alters our perspective and can commit to the "I trust" that Paul so confidently declares.

PHILIPPIANS 2:25

But I think it is necessary to send back to you Epaphroditus, my brother, coworker and fellow soldier, who is also your messenger, whom you sent to take care of my needs.

God grants us a familial relationship through Jesus that connects us as brothers and sisters (Hebrews 2:10-11). We are part of the same heavenly family and share an inheritance (1 Peter 1:3-5). So why do we expend so much energy striving for more than the person serving next to us?

We are coworkers with Christ (John 17:18) and members of His Body (1 Corinthians 12:27). So why do we compete against each other and complain about where he's placed us? We fight the same Enemy (John 17:15) and own the same promise of winning the fight as long as we fight together (John 17:22-23). So why do we struggle and strive against one another for a position on the battlefield?

Epaphroditus was an encouraging gift from the Philippians to Paul. He became Paul's brother, close companion in Gospel ministry, and a friend who endured worldly abuse together with Paul. He didn't compete for attention, or wonder if anyone noticed all he was doing. He partnered with and supported Paul. Their relationship is a perfect model of the kind of relationship we all should share.

PHILIPPIANS 2:26-28

For he longs for all of you and is distressed because you heard he was ill. Indeed he was ill and almost died. But God had mercy on him, and not on him only but also on me, to spare me sorrow upon sorrow. Therefore I am all the more eager to send him, so that when you see him again you may be glad and I may have less anxiety.

These verses give us a glimpse into the personal struggles that shaped Paul's trust in God and provided him with practical examples of faith. He expounded more fully in his letters to other churches, declaring that nothing could separate us from the love of God because he experienced that truth personally (Romans 8:37-39). He taught us to find contentment in simple things (1 Timothy 6:7-8) because we look forward to an unimaginable inheritance in heaven (1Peter 1:3-5). He modeled unshakable rejoicing in great suffering because he learned to rejoice under the weight of great sorrow (2 Corinthians 6:4-10).

Paul's faith did not spare him from struggling with worry or sadness over the suffering of others. He loved his coworkers dearly and felt distressed when they were distressed. But it did give him the means to bear up under strain and stand steadfastly upon the unshakable promises of God (2 Corinthians 1:3-6).

PHILIPPIANS 2:29-30

So then, welcome him in the Lord with great joy, and honor people like him, because he almost died for the work of Christ. He risked his life to make up for the help you yourselves could not give me.

Every person who commits themselves fulltime to Gospel ministry needs an Epaphroditus; a loving, selfless partner, who addresses their needs as they tend to the needs of others. Even the fittest pastor falters without such encouragement (1 Thessalonians 5:12-13). Epaphroditus was an invaluable part of Paul's active ministry, and Paul encourages the Philippians to show people like him honor.

Often, it is the pastor's wife who acts as Epaphroditus in our present-day churches. She attends to the needs of her husband so that he can minister faithfully. She sacrifices time with him, carries the largest load at home, and steadfastly encourages him when it difficult to bear up under the weight of ministry. So, it follows that she, like Epaphroditus, should be greeted with great joy and honored for her faithfulness. But too often, she experiences thanklessness, criticism, and complaints.

We can show our appreciation for our pastors' wives by offering an enthusiastic greeting on Sunday morning and an occasional heartfelt note of thanks. Such small blessings take the sting out of sacrifice and add joy to her service. (1 Thessalonians 5:11)

PHILIPPIANS 3:1

Further, my brothers and sisters, rejoice in the Lord! It is no trouble for me to write the same things to you again, and it is a safeguard for you.

Rejoicing in the Lord means leaning toward God as he leans toward you. It's the idea of being delighted to see or hear from a dear loved one or running into loving arms. Joy, like this, rests on God's character, not on circumstances or possessions. (Psalm 103:8)

Joy works in our relationships with one another too. Paul firmly encourages it in previous verses (Philippians 2:1-4). Authentic joy is a byproduct of genuine concern, humble service, and ready forgiveness (1 Corinthians 13:4-8). The caveat is that interpersonal rejoicing only works if each of us is trustworthy, gracious, and dependable (1 Peter 4:8).

PHILIPPIANS 3:2-3

Watch out for those dogs, those evildoers, those mutilators of the flesh. For it is we who are the circumcision, we who serve God by his Spirit, who boast in Christ Jesus, and who put no confidence in the flesh

There are always religious people who substitute their ideas of righteous living for God's. They look at others with critical eyes and listen with judging ears, waiting for an opportunity to catch someone else in sin. Often, their arrogant behavior hides some unconfessed sin of their own (Matthew 23:27).

We aren't saved by staunchly adhering to a particular set of expectations. Religious self-righteousness is simply worldliness dressed in pretty, church clothes. Jesus paid the entire price to save us (1 Peter 2:24). Our confidence rests in the finished work of Christ (Ephesians 2:8-9).

God is the only one who has the right to judge sin (James 4:12). In laying our sin on Jesus, he freed us from the crushing weight of religious expectations. Then he filled us with His Spirit, enabling us to express our gratitude to him through good works that reflect Jesus and not the flesh (1 Corinthians 6:19-20).

PHILIPPIANS 3:4-6

Though I myself could have such confidence. If anyone else thinks
he has grounds for confidence in the flesh, I have more:
circumcised on the eighth day, of the people of Israel, of the tribe
of Benjamin; a Hebrew of Hebrews; as to the law,
a Pharisee; as to zeal, persecuting the church;
as to righteousness in the law, faultless.

How is success in life measured? The Pharisees measured it by the accuracy of their religious performance—the more ticks on their 613-law checklist, the greater their love for God. Quite a few of us measure ourselves, and others, by a similarly misguided standard. (Galatians 5:4)

Jesus called the Pharisees "whited sepulchers" or whitewashed tombs (Matthew 23:27) because, for all their efforts, they still fell short of God's standard for holiness. We do too. (Romans 3:23)

But Jesus sacrificed himself to free us from harsh religious standards like those of the Pharisees. He performed flawlessly, so we never have to. He challenged works-based practices and overcame them to release us from such bondage (Galatians 5:1). He redefined the requirements of a godly life and opened the possibility of bringing God glory to all of us. He met God's expectation of holiness, the only one that counts, and then offered his righteousness in place of our failure to obey, making us cherished children of God (Romans 8:15).

PHILIPPIANS 3:7

But whatever was gain to me I count as loss for the sake of Christ.

It's difficult for our Western sensibilities to accept that the things we value most in life pale in comparison to knowing Jesus. The world bombards us with things that feed our tastes and appetites and promise to make us feel content. Worldly thought brainwashes us into believing that we can be the center of the universe. But the universe has only one center, and it is not us. We lack the foreknowledge to steer our destiny across the street, much less into eternity (Proverbs 16:9).

We were created and fulfilled by Christ. In him, we live, and move, and have our being (Acts 17:28). Outside of a relationship with Jesus, all our accomplishments are straw houses. Any move forward is wasted. (1 Corinthians 3:11-13). Paul understood this. That's why he willingly offered anything he had for the sake of Gospel ministry. Paul trusted God to restore the things he sacrificed richly. He had faith that there were better things ahead. (Hebrews 6:10)

PHILIPPIANS 3:8

---

*What is more, I consider everything a loss because of the
surpassing worth of knowing Christ Jesus my Lord, for whose sake
I have lost all things. I consider them garbage,
that I may gain Christ*

Secular society and some Christian camps bombard us with the lie
that stuff satisfies. Telling people that their walk with Christ will
be rich with material blessings is sinful. Christ's own walk makes it
clear that this is untrue. (Luke 9:58) We live in a fallen world rife
with the consequences of sin, and Christians are affected like
everyone else.

If anyone should have been comfortable and wealthy, it was Paul.
He was a zealous Pharisee, superior in his adherence to religious
law, a chief persecutor of the Early Church, and a Roman citizen.
(Philippians 3:3-6, Acts 22:3-5) But Paul considered his earthly
standing garbage compared to the eternal riches of knowing Christ.
Paul understood that the real treasure in life is a vibrant, full
relationship with God, no matter what the consequences (1 Peter
5:8-10)

PHILIPPIANS 3:9

And be found in him, not having a righteousness of my own that comes from the law, but that which is through faith in Christ—the righteousness that comes from God on the basis of faith.

Our heavenly standing does not depend on our own opinions, efforts, or understanding. It rests on the finished work of Jesus Christ. (Ephesians 2:4-5) When God looks at us, He sees us through the beautiful tapestry of every right word, act, and righteous judgment Jesus' ever made. (Galatians 3:27) His perfect obedience eternally supersedes our bad experiences, wrong choices, and failures. His character, displayed in us, becomes my righteousness, holiness, and redemption. (1 Corinthians 1:30)

Such knowledge is a game changer! Who we were yesterday does not negate who we choose to be today. We are free to grow in grace. We can look at things with fresh eyes and display Christ's righteousness authentically by our behavior. Through faith in Christ, we become more and more like him. God gives us the power to do just that. He multiplies his grace as we practice Christlikeness. (2 Peter 1:2-3)

PHILIPPIANS 3:10-11

I want to know Christ—yes, to know the power of his resurrection and participation in his sufferings, becoming like him in his death, and so, somehow, attaining to the resurrection from the dead.

There is no resurrection without death, no transformed body, no pile of grave clothes, no empty tomb, or experience of God's incredible power. We all lose without Christ's willing sacrifice of his own life. (Colossians 1:21-22)

Paul recognized that enjoying the benefits of Christ's great sacrifice without experiencing his suffering is understanding half the story. He carried our pain so we could support others in theirs and died for us so that we could live in sacrificial obedience to him. He took our sin upon himself, so we could help others be free. (2 Corinthians 5:17-18)

Experiencing the full power of the resurrection means dying to ourselves and allowing Christ to transform us. It means trading the ugly grave clothes of our sinfulness for the glorious garment of his perfect righteousness and walking out of the tomb of stubborn selfishness into a world waiting to hear Good News. (1 Peter 2:24)

PHILIPPIANS 3:12

*Not that I have already obtained all this, or have already arrived
at my goal, but I press on to take hold of that
for which Christ Jesus took hold of me.*

Our salvation is one and done. We acknowledge that we have sinned and fall short of God's glory (Romans 3:23) and that Jesus died a sinner's death so that we could live in peace with God (Romans 5:1-2). The security of his sacrifice is ours forever (Romans 8:38-39).

But that's just the beginning of the adventure. As the gratitude that such mercy and security wells up inside us, we are meant to express it in real and proper worship as God transforms us into the image of our Savior (Romans 12:1-2).

It is a lifelong journey full of peaks and valleys. Paul understood the necessity of pressing on through obstacles and failures to arrive at our spiritual destination. Our goal is God's glory and not our perfection, which no amount of effort on our part could ever obtain (Ephesians 2:8-9). The key to perseverance is an unshakeable understanding of who we are in Christ (1 Peter 2:9).

PHILIPPIANS 3:13-14

Brothers and sisters, I do not consider myself yet to have taken hold of it. But one thing I do: Forgetting what is behind and straining toward what is ahead, I press on toward the goal to win the prize for which God has called me heavenward in Christ Jesus.

It doesn't take long to grow weary of this world and bone-tired of its nonsense. The evil that surrounds us is overwhelming at times. But a little change in perspective can do wonders for a world-weary soul.

This world is not our destination, but a long, challenging hike to our real home. We can fix our gaze on our earthly surroundings and feed the habit of identifying the next obstacle before it arrives. We can expend valuable energy to control our environment and the people in it. Or we can fix our eyes on Jesus and leave the management of things to him. (Hebrews 12:1-2)

It's not easy to trust at that level, but it is healthy. Faith that God has things in hand is the best antidote for anxiety and fear (1 Peter 5:7). Lasting peace comes when we grab hold of the Gospel and hold on for dear life (John 16:33), trusting in its promises and relying on the knowledge that God sees, understands, and is working all things together for our good and his glory. (Romans 8:28)

PHILIPPIANS 3:15

All of us, then, who are mature should take such a view of things.
And if on some point you think differently,
that too God will make clear to you.

Christians don't have to think alike on every point to be bound together by the essential points. Sometimes we will disagree. It's okay to think differently if our opinion on one part of Scripture lines up with the rest of it, and we are honestly seeking God's view on a subject, not peddling a personal agenda (1 Corinthians 2:12-13). Discussion about the finer points sharpens our thinking and challenges our resolve. But it is never healthy to fall upon the tiny swords of hubris while lost people fall all around us (Romans 16:17-18).

God is the author of Truth, not us. He guards the authenticity of his Word and is fully capable of changing a person's point of view without our help. We've lost the ability to discuss without attacking (Ephesians 4:29), wasting so much time sparring with one another, rather than uniting to share God's Good News (Romans 15:5-7).

PHILIPPIANS 3:16

Only let us live up to what we have already attained.

It is easy to grow complacent in our walk with God. The world encroaches in its subtle way, wearing down our resolve and captivating us in a tyranny of choices that have very little to do with Grace and a lot to do with pride and position (Matthew 16:23).

We are so busy maintaining temporal lives that the miracle of our eternal life gets lost in the fray. We are rushed and harried to the point that we can't complete a regular conversation, much less a spiritual one (Matthew 6:19-20)

Paul reminds us that our salvation is a gift that moves with us rather than a point in time from which we move away. Our relationship with God elevates our involvement in life from ordinary to eternal. Every choice reflects either appreciation or ingratitude. Nothing we say or do is inconsequential. From the moment of salvation on, we represent our Savior (Ephesians 4:22-24).

PHILIPPIANS 3:17

Join together in following my example, brothers and sisters, and just as you have us as a model, keep your eyes on those who live as we do.

Paul modeled a Christ-like life for others. His walk with God stood in stark contrast with his walk without God. Faith changed him. Where once he took pride in his earthly accomplishments, which included zealous persecution of Christians, now he lived a humble life of self-sacrifice, serving others for the sake of the Gospel (Acts 20:18-21).

How do our present lives of faith contrast with our lives before we became Christians? Do our actions and choices because of Christ contrast sharply with those before we knew him (Colossians 3:1-17)? Are we comfortable encouraging others to follow our example as we follow Christ?

If our goal is to point others to their Savior, then our faith-lives must display a difference (Matthew 5:16). When people notice us, they should recognize our love for one another and our commitment to introducing Christ to the world (1 Peter 2:12). It's either that or confirming the erroneous belief that Christianity is impotent and faith in God makes no difference.

PHILIPPIANS 3:18-19

For, as I have often told you before and now tell you again even with tears, many live as enemies of the cross of Christ. Their destiny is destruction, their God is their stomach, and their glory is in their shame. Their mind is set on earthly things.

Enemies of the Cross should be easy to identify. They concentrate on earthly things like the acquisition of material possessions, the attainment of worldly accolades, and comfortable lives. They spend their best energy in pursuit of secular security and have hardly anything leftover for issues of faith or eternity (1 Corinthians 2:14).

You can identify them by the content of their conversations, which overflow with incivility and conceit (Matthew 12:34). They assume rather than listen and disparage those who don't agree with them. They justify hatefulness and treat others with contempt (Psalm 14:1).

If we are not diligent in our commitment to Christ, then we can fall so easily into this pattern of living, reflecting the world rather than the image of God within us (Ephesians 4:22-24). Our spitefulness overshadows God's grace. Our selfishness steals his glory.

PHILIPPIANS 3:20-21

But our citizenship is in heaven. And we eagerly await a Savior from there, the Lord Jesus Christ, who, by the power that enables him to bring everything under his control, will transform our lowly bodies so that they will be like his glorious body.

Our heavenly citizenship does not begin the day we die. Our residency changes then, but we are citizens of heaven from the minute we recognize Jesus as our Lord and Savior. Such a remarkable, eternal truth challenges our secular point of view. We are pilgrims, sojourners, no longer bound by earthly entanglements, headed toward eternity with direction and purpose (Hebrews 12:1-3).

Jesus applies every bump and trial, every joy and triumph for our transformation from selfish to sanctified. He leads us heavenward and strengthens our sense of urgency because every moment is significant, and every interaction is eternal (Colossians 3:23-24.)

PHILIPPIANS 4:1

Therefore, my brothers and sisters, you whom I love and long for, my joy and crown, stand firm in the Lord in this way, dear friends!

Jesus endured the Cross for the joy set before him (Hebrews 12:2) He didn't wander from the path. He didn't hesitate or complain. Jesus planted his feet and trusted that the direction God pointed was right and perfect. He stood firm because he had the faith to believe God's promise of better things ahead. Paul encourages us to do the same.

Our wandering feet grow weary and accompanied by drifting thoughts and wavering resolve. We are quick to look for a different way, one that fits our plans and feeds our selfish desires. We forget that Jesus earned this place for us on the road to Glory. (Isaiah 53:6)

The wide way of the world may seem better, with so much company and no firm direction. (Matthew 7:13) But, we walk the safest road, hand in hand with an experienced Guide who has traveled before us and knows the way. (John 14:6)

PHILIPPIANS 4:2-3

I plead with Euodia and I plead with Syntyche to be of the same mind in the Lord. Yes, and I ask you, my true companion, help these women since they have contended at my side in the cause of the gospel, along with Clement and the rest of my co-workers, whose names are in the book of life.

We don't have to agree with everyone on every issue. That would be impossible. But, as women of God, there is an expectation that we won't be contentious, unforgiving, or rude in our disagreement.

Paul entreated Euodia and Syntyche to agree in the Lord, a reminder to them and us that our relationship with Jesus is our common ground. It is the stout cord that binds us to one another, whether we agree or not. Satan tempts us to bicker about temporal things or push against one another to get our way. But, no matter what the issue, we are indebted to the same Savior, and we bear witness to the same Gospel. (Ephesians 4:29-32)

Unity between women is a serious business. Any break in the relationship between sisters in Christ affects the whole Body. We may not be able to agree on all things. But every one of us should be willing to relinquish our wishes and opinions for God's glory and the strength of our witness. (Romans 15:5-6)

PHILIPPIANS 4:4

Rejoice in the Lord always. I will say it again: Rejoice!

The Greek root of *rejoicing* is related to the word *grace*. Grace is God leaning toward us to bestow benefits. Rejoicing is leaning toward him to receive them. It's like a scene in the story of the prodigal son. Our Heavenly Father rushes forward to lavish us with blessings, and we run with joy to receive them (Luke 15:20).

What a beautiful picture! The great, generous, holy God, Lord of all things, wants to take care of us (James 1:17). There isn't anything or anyone that can prevent it! No circumstantial bully can bar his way! No doubt on our part negates his intent. It may rob us of experiencing joy in his provision, but it does not keep him from giving.

The key to joy in life is leaning toward God. It makes perfect sense when we think about who we are tilting toward. No matter how the world around us characterizes God, no matter what lies tempt us to lean away, His Word tells us that He is merciful, forgiving, good, and loving (Psalm 145:8-9), and his arms are open wide.

PHILIPPIANS 4:5

Let your gentleness be evident to all. The Lord is near.

It is easy to be swept away by the tide of disgruntled discontent in our world. We tend to bludgeon one another with opinion rather than encouraging each other with the Truth. Not personal truth (small "t"), but Gospel Truth (capital "T"), found only in God's Word – and even it can be a club in stubborn, selfish hands! Fearful people force. Gentle people lead.

Gentle people live in ways that fit the Gospel. They are wise, merciful, impartial, and sincere (James 3:17). Their strength comes from the example Christ lived out before them (Mark 2:15-17). They recognize that the power to help others think Biblically is God's alone and does not depend on any strong argument or loud debate. Gentle people communicate the Gospel best by their example (1 Peter 2:12) and by answering questions that arise when others see their faith in action (1 Peter 3:15-16).

PHILIPPIANS 4:6-7

Do not be anxious about anything, but in every situation, by prayer and petition, with thanksgiving, present your requests to God. And the peace of God, which transcends all understanding, will guard your hearts and your minds in Christ Jesus.

Anxiety is the overwhelming feeling of being swamped by circumstances. It's the pressure of needing to have a finger in every pot or attempting to manipulate every situation toward the desired outcome while trying to please everyone involved. It's classic, codependent behavior and is unhealthy for everyone (Matthew 6:27).

God assigns work in His Kingdom that is uniquely suited to each of us (1 Corinthians 12:7). Anxiety comes when we try to manage more than He intends. Paul urges us to let go of things we have no business holding, to settle into where God has placed us, and let others deal with their assignments unencumbered by our interference (1 Corinthians 12:15-18). Otherwise, we miss the incredible things God is doing in and around us.

We grow weary, discouraged, and anxious when we step into space that isn't our space because God has not equipped us to be there. But when we settle into where God wants us and invest time and energy in just what He has given us to do, then anxiety falls away, and we experience that deep, full breath we've been longing for but been too busy to take (Ephesians 4:11-13).

PHILIPPIANS 4:8

*Finally, brothers and sisters, whatever is true, whatever is noble,
whatever is right, whatever is pure, whatever is lovely, whatever
is admirable--if anything is excellent or praiseworthy—
think about such things.*

There is value to the words we speak if and only if they reflect the true nature of the Gospel. Anything else we say is empty, ugly, and sinful. Rudeness, sarcasm, labeling others - such dialogue reveals the hardness of our hearts. It is better to remain silent than to dishonor God with what we say. "For the mouth speaks what the heart is full of." (Matthew 12:34)

There's no getting around it. If bitterness, frustration, impatience, or judgment pass our lips, then they flow directly from the sinful hearts within us. But our speech changes when we take every thought captive (2 Corinthians 10:5). As we focus our attention as Paul directs in this verse, then sloppy and hurtful habits of expression make way for Gospel kindness and encouragement. When our mouths speak, they speak in truer, nobler tones. Our comments build rather than break.

God promises that we will give an account for the words we speak. No conversation remains hidden from his scrutiny. He is not tolerant of coarse joking or sloppy speech. "But I tell you that everyone will have to give account on the day of judgment for every empty word they have spoken." (Matthew 12:36)

PHILIPPIANS 4:9

Whatever you have learned or received or heard from me or seen in me—put it into practice.

Our human nature seeks distraction from personal inadequacies by focusing on the perceived strength of others. The world is rife with hero worship for that very reason. The public lives of movie stars, athletes, superheroes, politicians fascinate us and fill our minds with false ideas of what it means to be exceptional. Directing our attention outside ourselves diverts the necessity of looking within.

But we are in Christ, and our heavenly nature seeks a different kind of hero. Paul urges the Philippians to be like him, not because he is exceptional, but because the image of Christ that he lives out before them is (1 Corinthians 11:1). Godly heroes always point us to Christ.

Exceptional by God's definition is different than the world's definition. It means present, available, trusting, and willing to live for his glory and not our own, and the people we chose to emulate should excel in those qualities (Hebrews 12:1).

PHILIPPIANS 4:10

I rejoiced greatly in the Lord that at last you renewed your concern for me. Indeed, you were concerned, but you had no opportunity to show it.

Personal support of Gospel ministry reflects the priority we place on it. It does. Kingdom work flourishes when Christians give generously of their time, talents, and resources. It diminishes when we do not.

We show concern by directing our hearts and minds toward heavenly priorities and forsaking the world (Colossians 3:1-3). That means jumping at the opportunity to serve God by serving others, without the usual excuses and qualifiers (Ephesians 6:7).

This kind of Gospel generosity requires planning so that God gets the best of our resources and not the leftovers (1 Peter 2:4-5). It requires surrendering ourselves as an act of worship to the one who sacrificed everything for us (Romans 12:1) and not withholding when we can give. (Proverbs 3:27)

PHILIPPIANS 4:11-12

I am not saying this because I am in need, for I have learned to be content whatever the circumstances. I know what it is to be in need, and I know what it is to have plenty. I have learned the secret of being content in any and every situation, whether well fed or hungry, whether living in plenty or in want.

When sin entered the world, it brought consequences with it, consequences that we'll experience until Christ returns. But that doesn't mean we should be overwhelmed by them. Hunger, heartache, want, and plenty are a part of everyday life. The secret is knowing how to live with daily struggles without letting them overwhelm our faith (Romans 8:31).

God never guarantees the absence of pain, suffering, or loss in this lifetime. He does, however, offer peace, joy, and comfort as we experience them. God does not promise prosperity, but he does promise to meet our needs, the most important of which is a vibrant, active, faith-filled relationship with him (Psalm 23:1).

Every trial and hardship we face draws us closer to God, every blessing too. Our best lives don't rest on our material possessions or problem-free days. We are most contented and satisfied once we accept the fact that God is enough, no matter our circumstances (1 John 4:4).

PHILIPPIANS 4:13

I can do all this through him who gives me strength.

We can't accomplish everything we set out to do, despite what the sneaker companies tell us. Our strength is finite and will eventually fail us no matter how hard we work to increase it. Our capacity is limited, and there will someday be a challenge too great for us to overcome.

But God's strength is undefeatable (Ephesians 1:16-21), and he promises to equip us for any task he sets before us (1 Timothy 1:12). We are strong in his mighty power. (Ephesians 6:10). We may not be able to accomplish everything we want to achieve, but we can surely complete any task God assigns (2 Corinthians 4:7). The Holy Spirit fortifies our insufficiency and strengthens our feeble efforts (Ephesians 3:14-19), so we produce a harvest of righteousness for God's glory and not our own (Colossians 1:29).

PHILIPPIANS 4:14-16

Yet it was good of you to share in my troubles. Moreover, as you Philippians know, in the early days of your acquaintance with the gospel, when I set out from Macedonia, not one church shared with me in the matter of giving and receiving, except you only; for even when I was in Thessalonica, you sent me aid more than once when I was in need.

The Philippians made missional support a priority. Paul commended them for their faithful giving. They were exceptional friends to him from the first moments they received the Gospel, facilitating his outreach to other communities. They gave sacrificially, trusting that there would be an eternal return on their investment (Luke 6:38).

Those committed to careers in Gospel ministry need that same exceptional support. They work steadfastly, with the goals of the Kingdom in mind, while the rest of us tend to fit ministry around personal priorities when it is convenient and comfortable. If those called to ministry careers do work outside their ministry, it is to support further ministry in the place God has called them. But their hearts hold a hope that their Christian family will give so generously that they can forego the distraction of secular employment (2 Corinthians 9:10-12).

Consider being an exceptional friend to someone in fulltime ministry. Encourage them by your enthusiastic support of their work and by generously giving to alleviate the distraction of meeting daily needs.

PHILIPPIANS 4:17-18

Not that I desire your gifts; what I desire is that more be credited to your account. I have received full payment and have more than enough. I am amply supplied, now that I have received from Epaphroditus the gifts you sent. They are a fragrant offering, an acceptable sacrifice, pleasing to God.

If you ever wonder what it takes to please God, be generous. Open-hearted, open-handed giving is always sweet-smelling, fully acceptable, and entirely pleasing to him. Nothing reflects his image more accurately. God loves a cheerful giver! (2 Corinthians 9:7)

But don't expect a pat on the back (Matthew 6:3). The phrase "credited to your account" didn't mean that the Philippians would improve their heavenly standing before God by giving, or that it earned them favor. Paul encouraged them by assuring them that their gift to his ministry would have a more significant impact than they could ever imagine. Their offering was useful, adequate, and appreciated.

Those who, like Paul, commit to Gospel ministry as a career depend on God for their daily bread, but recognize that God works through other Christians to provide it. The generosity of the Church is foundational to active Gospel ministry. God abundantly gives so we can give generously (1 Timothy 6:18) and multiplies our giving to accomplish his work in the world. (2 Corinthians 9:10-11)

PHILIPPIANS 4:19

*And my God will meet all your needs according
to the riches of his glory in Christ Jesus.*

Our media crazed world bombards us with false ideas about what is necessary for a contented and happy life. Advertisers are so relentless that it can be difficult to distinguish between a genuine need and a programmed want. If we are not careful, worldly messages seep into our thoughts and take residence, and we exhaust ourselves running after things that will never satisfy (2 Corinthians 9:8).

Without a relationship with God, my greatest need remains unmet. I need a Savior. Every other need stems from that one. God's forgiveness, grace, and mercy are vital. Most of the rest is fluff and nonsense. (John 6:27)

Consistent prayer and regular Bible study help distinguish between real needs and twaddle (Ephesians 1:17-18). If we fill our thoughts with God's thoughts, then there will be no room for worldly nonsense that can never satisfy, no matter what advertisers want us to believe.

PHILIPPIANS 4:20

To our God and Father be glory for ever and ever. Amen.

Paul just finished encouraging the Philippians to be living examples of faith in their character (Philippians 4:1), conversation (Philippians 4:4), and conduct (Philippians 4:9). Paul understood the importance of living as Jesus lived. Jesus modeled perfect obedience (John 15:10), his every conversation pointed others toward God's truth (John 7:18), and he expended his best energy doing the work the Father sent him to do. (John 17:4).

We are reflectors of Jesus. The integrity of our message rests on how accurately we display him to the world. Since Jesus was obedient to the Father, we must be obedient to the Father all the time and not just when it is easy or convenient. Because he placed a high priority on proclaiming God's Word, we need to cultivate speech that is rich in God's Truth. Since he spent his best efforts every day doing heavenly business, our activities every minute of every day should reflect the same priority. Our purpose on earth is to glorify God. Everything else in our lives should be the means to do it.

PHILIPPIANS 4:21-22

Greet all God's people in Christ Jesus. The brothers and sisters who are with me send greetings. All God's people here send you greetings, especially those who belong to Caesar's household.

It's important to remember that God's mandate is to go and share the Gospel (Mark 16:15). That means stepping out of our comfort zones. It might even mean living "in Caesar's household" - those hard and secular spots of society that lack awareness of God at all.

Think of it this way, what if all the doctors decided to stay in medical school? What if they built a private building and met there a couple of times a week to discuss medicine? What if their conversations hinged around the value of practicing medicine and how necessary it was for the sick people outside their walls, but they failed to step out of doors to practice it? What if they decided that the safest course was to remain separate from the people who needed them? That would be tragic and silly (Matthew 5:13-14).

We are stewards of the life-giving message of the Great Physician, who came to earth because sin-sick people need hope and healing (Luke 5:31). But we must interact with infected people to be able to administer healing grace.

PHILIPPIANS 4:23

The grace of the Lord Jesus Christ be with your spirit. Amen.

Philippians begins and ends with sweet, clean, and restorative Grace that chases away the suffocating air of worldliness and replaces it with brisk, invigorating Gospel Truth (Philippians 1:9-11). Grace restores our spirit when worldly thought sucks us dry. It allows us to live freely and fully in God's presence no longer held captive by unhealthy ideas and attitudes (Philippians 2:14-16). Because of Jesus, we have a filter that protects us from choking on the ugliness around us and provides a rich source of Grace-breath that enlivens us, so we can put our all into glorifying God and obeying his will (Philippians 3:20-21). Through Him, we have joy and peace with God forever (Philippians 4:4-7)